*What Jesus
Had to Say
About Money*

THE KING'S INSTITUTE
THE CHURCH ON THE WAY

3/20/06

11-5-07

B. C.

What Jesus Had to Say About Money

by

FRANK C. LAUBACH

ZONDERVAN PUBLISHING HOUSE
GRAND RAPIDS   MICHIGAN

WHAT JESUS HAD TO SAY ABOUT MONEY

Contents

A Preliminary Word

Any man smart enough and practical enough to make a fortune, is not satisfied to leave in doubt the most important question of all—his own eternal fate. This is why many intelligent Christians of large means, when they approach their last days on earth, are plagued with misgivings by the words of Jesus:

"How hard it will be for those who have riches to enter the kingdom of God" (Mark 10:23, RSV; Matthew 19:23; Luke 18:24). "My children, how hard it is to enter the kingdom of God."

His astonished disciples asked: "Who then can be saved?"

Jesus replied: "With men it is impossible, but with God all things are possible."

Not only the millionaires are included in that hard saying, but most of the rest of us. Anyone with a bank account or property worth $10,000 is a rich man, compared to the vast majority of the world's population. Half the world has no bank account and no property — only debt. Everyone with an automobile and a house is "rich."

We who approach our final years want to know just what Jesus thinks of us. Does He count us in, or does He count us out? It is a question which we usually avoid discussing, and preachers seldom mention it. But what could be more cruel than to permit old or sickly people to go through the valley of the shadow of death all alone, afraid to face the final Judge? Every rich man or woman in America is on my conscience until I have tried to help him answer his last and biggest question. We will study the question together — what does the Lord say?

Fortunately, if one reads all the teachings of Jesus carefully, the answer is plain as day. It is always the same answer, and it is thrilling beyond our wildest expectations — if we do what Jesus asks.

The rich man supposes that he cannot take his wealth with him when he dies. But Jesus says this is untrue. The rich man can send his wealth on ahead of him, and find it waiting for him when he arrives in the Kingdom of Heaven; this is what Jesus declares.

But how does one lay up such "a bank account in heaven"? Jesus tells us how, over and over, and His teaching is always the same. It can be summarized like this:

Whatever you do to help people who are in want and misery, is laid up as your treasure in heaven. On the other hand, what you refuse to do to help people in want and misery is recorded on the red side of the ledger account, against you on the day of Judgment, and this can keep you out. Jesus tells us with terrifying vividness in Matthew 25:31-46. You may want to turn to your Bible and read it.

Jesus says it even more briefly and sharply in Luke 12:33:

"Sell your possessions, and use your money to help needy people. In this way you will provide for yourself wealth in heaven that does not

9

fail, where no thief can get near it, no moth destroy it" (paraphrased).

Nothing in the teachings of Jesus is more emphasized or better illustrated.

It is exactly what we would expect of Jesus. His heart overflowed with compassion for people in trouble. He spent every hour of every day seven days a week, relieving suffering and saving the lost.

When He returned to Nazareth, His boyhood home, He stood up in the synagogue and read these words from Isaiah:

"The Spirit of the Lord is upon me,
He has consecrated me to preach the good
news to the poor;
He has sent me to heal the broken hearted,
To announce release to captives,
And recovery of sight to the blind,
And liberty to those who are oppressed;
To proclaim the year acceptable to the Lord."

He sat down and told them: "This passage is being fulfilled in your presence today." That was the platform, the program and life work of Jesus. When we help the hungry, the broken hearted, the captives, the oppressed, we help Him, and He says we shall enter His Kingdom (see Matthew 9:36-38).

Some person may object: "I thought the Bible said: 'Believe on the Lord Jesus Christ and thou shalt be saved.' " Yes, but obeying Him is the crucial test of whether we really believe Him. All of us judge people by what they *do*. Jesus says plainly: "Not everyone who says to me, 'Lord, Lord' will get into the Kingdom of Heaven, but only those who do the will of my Father in heaven."

"You are my friends if you do whatever I command you" (John 15:14).

"If you keep my commandments, you will abide in my love" (John 15:10).

Jesus judges us, not by our professions or our promises, but our deeds. There is no doubt about that.

Now shall we together examine the life and teachings of Jesus to see whether it is true that compassion for the unfortunates is indeed always "the key to the kingdom"?

11

What Jesus Had to Say About Money

We may start with the occurrence which led Jesus to make His disturbing statement about how "hard it is for those who have riches to enter the Kingdom of Heaven."

The Rich Young Ruler

The Rich Young Ruler

A rich young ruler came running, knelt at the feet of Jesus, and asked Him, "Master, what good deed must I do to inherit eternal life?"

Jesus said to him: "If you want to inherit eternal life, keep the commandments."

He asked, "Which ones?"

Jesus named our duties toward our fellow-men: "You shall not murder; you shall not commit adultery; you shall not steal; Honor your father and mother; you shall love your neighbor as you do yourself."

The young man said to Him, "I have obeyed all these commandments from my youth. What do I still lack?"

Jesus looked at him and loved him, and said to him, "There is one thing you lack. If you

15

want to be perfect, go, sell your property and give the money to the poor and you will have riches in heaven. Then come back and be a follower of Mine."

The young man dropped his head and walked away, much cast down, for he was very rich.

Jesus looked at His disciples and said: "How hard it is for those who *have riches to enter the kingdom of God.*"

That is the incident. The young man had rejected not *one* offer but *two*. Jesus had shown him:

1. How to get to heaven.
2. How to "have riches in heaven."

By investing his wealth to help destitute people, Jesus declares this rich young man could have transferred his bank account from earth to heaven. "You will have riches in heaven."

This "investment in heaven" idea was central in the teachings of Jesus, repeated over and over, as you shall see in this book. In Matthew 6:19 the Lord says, "Do not store up your riches on earth, where moth and rust corrupt them, and where thieves break through and steal. But store up your riches in heaven, where moth and rust cannot destroy them, and where thieves cannot break through and steal them" (paraphrased).

There is not a word against *making* money —but a warning to be careful what bank you put it in! If it is in a bank on earth, it cannot last long, for either it will be stolen from you, or you will, when you die, be stolen from *it*— unless you have deposited it in heaven.

I used to suppose Jesus was saying, "Don't make money on earth," but He said no such thing. He was saying, "Take care what you do with it. Store it in heaven. What you give for meeting the sufferings of unfortunate people is your treasure, waiting for you in heaven. Make money, if you have a gift in that direction, and use it to meet human need."

But the rich young man turned away sadly, rejected the way Jesus offered him to get into heaven. He could not comprehend the strange paradox of Jesus: "What you give of life or money for human sufferers, you have forever in heaven" (Mark 10:21, paraphrased).

17

The young ruler went home and continued to keep the commandments as he had always done. He continued to go to the temple and pray, as he had always done, and to tithe and fast. He could have said with truth:

"O God, I thank You that I am not like other men, greedy, dishonest, or adulterous. I fast two days in the week; I pay tithes on everything I get" (Luke 18:11, 12 paraphrased).

He tried to earn eternal life by keeping the Jewish law and ritual. Ceremony instead of compassion.

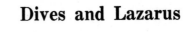

Dives and Lazarus

Dives and Lazarus

But, said Jesus, one thing the rich ruler omitted. He did nothing for a poor beggar named Lazarus, who lay outside his gate. Lazarus was full of sores, and so hungry that he was eager to eat what was thrown from the rich man's table. The dogs came and licked his sores. He died of disease and starvation, and was carried away by the angels to the bosom of Abraham (Luke 16:20-22).

Meanwhile the rich man (Dives by name) must have figured that God was on his side, for he continued to prosper. He used to dress in purple and fine linen, as rulers usually do, and he feasted sumptuously every day (Luke 16:19).

His lands yielded better than ever, the year

21

Lazarus died. He said to himself: "What am I going to do, for I have nowhere to store my crops? This is what I will do; I will tear down my barns and build larger ones, and in them I will store all my grain and my goods. Then I will say to my soul, 'Soul, you have great wealth stored up for years to come. Now take your ease, eat, drink and enjoy yourself.' " But, according to Jesus, God said to the rich ruler, "You fool, this very night your soul will be demanded of you. Who then will have all you have accumulated?"

"That is the way," Jesus added, "with the man who is not rich with God, but lays up his money for himself" (Luke 12:16-21; Mark 8:36, 37 paraphrased).

Dives may have died of a heart attack due to "feasting sumptuously every day"—while Lazarus lay starving outside his gate. He died of overeating while Lazarus died of malnutrition. He could not please God because he did not help Lazarus. He failed in his final examination at the Judgment Day. He did not get into heaven; he landed in hell. Jesus describes

22

his condition down below in terribly vivid language (Luke 16:23-31).

"Being in torment, Dives lifted up his eyes and saw Abraham far off, and Lazarus in his bosom. And he called out, 'Father Abraham, have mercy upon me, and send Lazarus to dip the tip of his finger in water and cool my tongue, for I am in torment here in these flames.' But Abraham said, 'Son, remember that in your lifetime you received your good things, and Lazarus had misfortunes in his; but now he is comforted here, while you are in anguish. There is a great chasm set between us, so that those who want to go over from this side to you cannot, and they cannot cross from your side to us.' Dives said, 'Then I beg you, Father Abraham, to send him to my father's house, for I have five brothers; let him warn them so that they will not also come to this place of torture.' Abraham answered, 'They have Moses and the prophets; let them listen to them.' But Dives said, 'No, Father Abraham, but if someone will go to them from the dead they will repent.' He answered, 'If they

will not hear Moses and the prophets, they
will not be convinced even if someone rises
from the dead' " (paraphrased).

That horrible story makes one shudder. But
it at once raises the question we are trying to
answer in this book: "Why was Dives in hell?"
Was it for being rich? If Abraham had sent
Lazarus back to the five brothers of Dives, what
would Lazarus have said? Would he have said,
"Repent for being rich"? No! Repent for
being hard-hearted.

Dives was in hell because he did not help
Lazarus. If those five brothers had read Moses
and the prophets they would have read no con-
demnation of being rich. They would have
read over and over a thousand times: "Have
mercy on the poor. Help those in need; share
with your brother; love your neighbor in deeds
as well as in words."

Jesus never reprimanded anyone for work-
ing diligently and for succeeding in his business. He praised industrious men, he condemned laziness (Luke 19:12-26). Jesus

judged men, not by the money they had earned, but by what they did with their money (and their lives) to relieve need.

Be grateful if you are rich, for this gives you greater power to relieve the destitute people of the world. Not riches, but a hard heart sends men to hell—whether they are rich or poor.

This is made so clear in Matthew 25:31-46 that even a child could not miss the point. It is the parable of the Last Judgment, the most dramatic and terrifying parable of them all.

The Last Judgment

The Last Judgment

"When the Son of Man comes in his splendor, and all his angels with him, he will take his seat on his glorious throne. All the nations will be gathered before him, and he will separate them from one another, just as a shepherd separates his sheep from his goats. He will put the sheep on his right hand, and the goats on his left.

"Then the king will say to those at his right, 'Come, you whom my Father has blessed. Take possession of the Kingdom which has been destined for you from the creation of the world. For when I was hungry, you gave me food. When I was thirsty, you gave me something to drink. When I was a stranger you invited me to your homes. When I had no clothing, you gave me clothes. When I was sick you visited me. When I was in prison, you came to see me.

"Then the upright will answer, 'Lord, when did we see you hungry and give you food; or thirsty and give you something to drink? When did we see you a stranger and invite you home; or without clothing and supply you with it? When did we see you sick or in prison, and go to see you?' The king will answer, 'I tell you, insofar as you did it to one of the humblest of these brothers of mine, you did it to me.'

"Then he will say to those at his left, 'Begone, you accursed people, to the everlasting fire destined for the Devil and his angels! For when I was hungry, you gave me nothing to eat; when I was thirsty, you gave me nothing to drink. When I was a stranger you did not invite me to your homes; when I had no clothes you did not supply me. When I was sick and in prison, you did not look after me.' They will answer, 'When did we see you hungry, or thirsty, or a stranger, or in need of clothes, or sick, or in prison, and did not wait upon you?' Then he will answer, 'I tell you, insofar as you failed to do it to one of these people who are humblest, you failed to do it for me.'

"They will go away to everlasting punishment, and the upright to everlasting life" (paraphrased).

Thus ends the most soul-searching parable in the Bible. It is awful; but we must admit that its meaning is crystal clear and powerful. The power of Jesus to convict men of sin lies in His relentless honesty.

At this dreadful Last Judgment we are not asked how rich or poor we were, but only: "What did you do for Lazarus?" It is enough to frighten us all. It leaves us all stricken with remorse, for we can all remember how often we have pushed people aside and hurried on without helping them. We who are not rich have used our lack of wealth as an excuse for refusing to listen to the plea for help. "Let those who can afford it do their part," is our alibi.

The Unforgiving Servant

The Unforgiving Servant

Jesus includes rich and poor alike. This is made clear in the parable of The Unforgiving Servant (Matthew 18:23-35).

"The Kingdom of heaven," said Jesus, "should be thought of in this way: There was once a king who decided to settle accounts with the men who served him. At the outset there was a man whose debt ran into the millions. Since he had no means of paying, his master ordered him to be sold to meet the debt, with his wife and children and everything he had. The man fell prostrate at his master's feet. 'Be patient with me,' he said, 'and I will pay in full.' The master was so moved with pity that he let the man go and remitted the debt.

"But no sooner had the man gone out than he met a fellow-servant who owed him twenty dollars; and catching hold of him he gripped him by the throat and said, 'Pay me what you owe.' The man fell at his fellow-servant's feet and begged him, 'Be patient with me, and I will pay you.' But he refused and had him jailed until he should pay the debt. The other servants were deeply distressed when they saw what had happened, and they went to their master and told him the whole story. He accordingly sent for the man. 'You scoundrel!' he said to him, 'I remitted the whole of your debt when you appealed to me; were you not bound to show your fellow-servant the same pity that I showed you?' And so angry was the master that he condemned the man to torture until he should pay the debt in full. And that is how your heavenly Father will deal with you, unless you each forgive your brother from your hearts" (Matthew 18:23-35 paraphrased).

36 If that were the last word, we all, rich and poor alike, would have reason to quail before

the thought of the Last Judgment. But thank God we have another chance. No matter what the past may have been, it can be wiped out, we can "turn over a new leaf," we can begin anew any hour. This is beautifully illustrated in the incident with Zacchaeus, told in Luke 19.

Zacchaeus

Zacchaeus

Jesus was passing through Jericho on the way to Jerusalem. Zacchaeus was the principal tax collector in Jericho, and a rich man. He wanted to see who Jesus was, but he could not see Him on account of the crowd, for he was a short man. So he ran on ahead and climbed up in a sycamore tree to see Him, for He was to pass that way. When Jesus came to the place, He looked up and said to him, "Zacchaeus, come down quickly, for I must stay at your house today."

Zacchaeus hurried down and welcomed Jesus joyfully. When the crowd saw this, they all complained and said, "He has gone to be the guest of a man who is a sinner."

But Zacchaeus stopped and said to Jesus,

"See, Master, I will give half my property to the poor; and if I have defrauded anyone of anything, I will pay him four times as much."

Jesus exclaimed: "Today salvation has come to this house. The Son of Man has come to seek and to save the lost" (Luke 19:1-10).

What had Zacchaeus said that led Jesus to declare that he was saved?

Zacchaeus had done what the rich young ruler did not do; what Dives in hell had failed to do. He gave half his wealth to meet the needs of the poor.

So, those who are rich like Zacchaeus, and who are approaching the last Judgment, have a wonderful answer to their question, "How can I put my house in order and be ready to face the Judge?" The answer is: "Invest your money in meeting the needs of destitute people. It will be waiting for you when you enter the kingdom."

It is never too late, so long as you have a tongue to speak, or a hand to wield a pen. You can send your wealth on ahead of you by investing it to relieve hunger and misery. If you do this, some day you may have the unspeakable joy of looking down over the parapets of heaven and watching your blessed influence go on and on for those whom Christ pities most; the dejected, the starving, the bewildered, who may be blessed for centuries after you have left this earth. They will rise up in the Judgment to thank you for what you have done.

There is something else wonderful about the teaching of Jesus. Even if a man's conscience worries him about money which he may have made at the expense of others, he can *redeem that money* by using it for compassion, and by righting the wrongs he feels he has done.

A large part of Zacchaeus' wealth was won by defrauding people; Zacchaeus himself admitted it; and every tax gatherer was doing it in his day. When Zacchaeus offered to repay fourfold those he had wronged, Jesus cried out in delight: "Salvation has come to his house."

This is the most wonderful "good news" in all the gospels—we can right the wrongs we have done, and start all over. It is the "good

43

news" about new beginnings. We can save
not only bad people, but "ill-gotten" money,
which we or our ancestors got by wrong doing.

Here is one of the most astonishing verses
in the whole world:

"Make friends for yourselves with your ill-
gotten wealth, so that when it fails, they may
take you into eternal dwellings!" (Luke 16:9).
Then Jesus adds these words: "If you are un-
trustworthy in using your ill-gotten wealth,
who will trust you with true riches?"

This astonishes us because it is so completely
opposite to the human idea of "justice," so
opposite to our entire legal system, which de-
mands punishment for crime.

It seems too good to be true. Yet it is in
harmony with the whole purpose of Jesus. He
came to help men turn over a new leaf, to right
the world's wrong, "God sent his Son into
the world, not to condemn the world, but that
the world through him might be saved" (John
3:17).

44   Jesus teaches us to pray, "Forgive us our
trespasses, as we forgive those who trespass

against us." God is forever eager to forgive and forget and start all over; so we see how the rich man can get into the kingdom—"all things are possible with God," even at the last hour of life. Because God is not watching for an opportunity to punish us, but to redeem us. "He takes no pleasure in the death of the wicked."

The Good Samaritan

The Good Samaritan

Perhaps the most loved of all the parables of Jesus is "The Good Samaritan" (Luke 10: 25-37). This parable gives precisely the same "key to the Kingdom of Heaven" as all the parables we have just quoted. A Lawyer came to ask Jesus:

"Teacher, what shall I do to inherit eternal life?"

Jesus asked him: "What is written in the law?"

The lawyer replied: 'Love the Lord with all your heart, and soul and strength and mind, and your neighbor as yourself."

Jesus said: "You have answered right; do this and you shall have eternal life."

The lawyer wanted to justify his actions, and so said, "Who is my neighbor?"

Then Jesus told him this famous parable:

"A man was going down from Jerusalem to Jericho, and he fell among robbers, who stripped him and beat him, and departed, leaving him half dead. Now by chance a priest was going down that road; when he saw him he passed by on the other side. So likewise a Levite, when he came to the place and saw him, passed by on the other side. But a Samaritan, as he journeyed, came to where he was; and when he saw him, he had compassion, and went to him and bound up his wounds, pouring in oil and wine; then he set him on his beast and brought him to an inn, and took care of him. And the next day he took out a dollar and gave it to the innkeeper, saying, 'Take care of him, and whatever you spend, I will repay you when I come back.'

"Which of these do you think proved neighbor to the man who had fallen among robbers?

"The lawyer said: 'The one who showed mercy on him.'

"Jesus said to him, 'Go, and do the same thing.' "

That was Jesus' answer to the lawyer's question: "What shall I do to inherit eternal life?" The answer was: Help *every* Lazarus!

That is a big order. *Half the world* has fallen among thieves, who have stripped them and left them half dead. Half the world *is* *Lazarus*. Half the world is going to bed tonight hungry. Help them and thou shalt have eternal life!

A Final Recap

A Final Recap

Most "rich young rulers" turn away from this order of Jesus. This is why it is "hard for them to enter the Kingdom of heaven." But it ought not to be hard for older men and women of wealth, who are in the twilight of life. Where can you put your hope save in the promises of Jesus? As Peter said to the Lord: "To whom else shall we go? Thou hast the words of eternal life."

So it should be easier for older people to get into the kingdom. Nothing stands in their way excepting the difficulty of breaking habits of a lifetime. They must reverse the habit of storing up in this world; they must invest their savings in human need before they leave this world, if they want it to be waiting for them in heaven.

This does not mean, recklessly or hastily

getting rid of all they have. John D. Rockefeller, Jr., was scrupulously conscientious and
careful about investing the millions which his
father had accumulated, where it would do the
maximum good. He understood the meaning
of those words of Jesus: "If you are untrust-
worthy in using your wealth, who will trust
you with true riches?" (Luke 16:11).

He devoted all his time to studying his be-
nevolences to make sure they would benefit
mankind. We, too, will want to be sure that
the channels we choose do really carry the
"water of life" out where people need it. We
do not want to support organizations which
use up their money in over-head, or for large
salaries. We have seen the heartache of our
government as it found its gifts going into
the pockets of the rich abroad, instead of helping the poor.

We also want to be sure that the relief we
give is not merely temporary, only postponing
the day of their starvation instead of ending
poverty. Not like Christmas dinners for the
poor, that forget them the rest of the year. Blind,

unwise charity may salve our own consciences, without doing any permanent good.

The only permanent cure is to educate the hungry ignorant half of the world to provide for themselves. Teach them in how to utilize the earth's soil and minerals to provide for their own needs; this is the only true and lasting cure. Not throwing crumbs or dimes at Lazarus, but healing his sores, and teaching him how to work for his own living, and to provide for a family — this is being "trustworthy" in giving away our money.

It takes wise, careful planning to arrange for your fortune to continue to bless all mankind for a thousand years, as the Rockefeller Foundation is doing.

This straightforward statement of what Jesus taught will be appreciated by practical business men; and God certainly approves it. If we "meet beyond the river" you may thank me for presenting accurately the *whole* teaching of Jesus about money, without attempting to explain anything away, or to cast doubt upon His authority.

57

What Jesus Had to Say About Money

No one is likely to present this matter before you so clearly and honestly again. If it is important, "do it now" is sound business practice.

Jesus says, "Pray that you may succeed in standing in the presence of the Son of Man. Take care—for fear he may come unexpectedly and find you asleep. What I am telling you I mean for all—be on the watch." Mark 13. "Now is the acceptable time."

James Russell Lowell in his powerful poem, "The Present Crisis," says:

> *Once to every man and nation*
> *Comes the moment to decide*
> *And the choice goes by forever . . .*
> *'Twixt that darkness and that light . . .*

For you this is the moment to decide. . . . And the choice some day goes by forever.

This book about "Jesus and Your Money" is incomplete. It is only one side of the story. For it would be a disastrous mistake to leave the impression that Jesus asks only our *money.* He asks also our *selves,* our thought, our time,

our way of life. To the rich young ruler, He
said:

"Give your money where it is needed, and ✳
come follow me." In other words, give your
life also, where it is needed. "Whoever," said
Jesus, "tries to save his life, shall lose it, and
whoever loses his life for my sake shall preserve it for eternal life." What does Jesus
mean? He cannot mean, "Go and get yourself killed in battle." Obviously he means "a
new way of life" when he says "life." Whoever tries to preserve his old way of life shall
lose it, and whoever leaves his old way of life
for my sake, shall preserve it for eternal life."
That makes sense. Jesus puts it still another
way: "If anyone wants to go with me, he must
disregard himself, take up his cross and follow me." The "cross" which we must take up
is to sacrifice our old selfish way of life, and
to seek "first the kingdom of God." To the
two fishermen, Jesus said, "Follow me, and
you will become fishers of men. Henceforth
it is men you will fish for." He called them   *59*
to follow a *new profession.*

So along with investing our money goes investing our lives.

Investing our *money* to meet human need, insures that the money is deposited in heaven, waiting for us. But if we are to go there to claim our "treasure" we must also invest ourselves.

Jesus, always reaching for vivid figures of speech, said, "You must be born again." Our reason for living is born again; our way of thinking, our use of time must be born again. After this new birth we spend our time helping him build his "Kingdom of heaven." This change of life, as radical as a new birth, is like living in a new country, or becoming a junior member of a new partnership.

Let us try to picture the "complete Christian" who fulfills the specifications which Jesus laid down for entrance into the Kingdom of God.

The completely involved Christian is interested in need *near at hand,* but also in need far away *across the wide oceans.* He can him-

60

self touch the people near him, but he must employ a proxy to do his work in far countries.

In other words he has *two feet,* one *at home* and the other *abroad.* He will help support one or more missionaries in some far country who will work with native Christians to help lift needy people and lead them to Christ. At home he will do this himself. He will be his own missionary. At home he will spend his *time* helping and winning people, abroad he will spend his *money.* At home his arm will reach *down,* abroad it will reach far *out.*

Every community has people who are beneath our social circle, whom we forget when we live for self but remember when we follow Jesus. He leads us down to seek the lost. He may be

    A foreigner who needs to learn English
    A native illiterate who needs to learn to read
    A drop-out or near drop-out in school
    A retarded person
    A juvenile delinquent
    An ex-prisoner seeking to come back
    A mentally disturbed person

An invalid or shut-in
An old lonesome has-been
A failure defeated by life
A wall flower

Christ constantly found some unlovable person who needed love. You and I can select
some such neglected person, plan repeated con-
tacts with him in classes or in conversations,
amaze him with our kindness, until he asks
us *why* we are being so kind, and then tell him
we are following Jesus.

That was the method of Jesus Himself. First
He astonished people by His deeds of compassion, and when they were "conditioned" to
listen to His words, He told them His "good
news." They would not have believed His
words if they had not seen His deeds. He lived
it before He said it. He *was* His gospel before
He proclaimed His gospel. Then when He
spoke, they knew what He meant, for they
had seen it in His eyes and acts.

62 How, in our sophisticated and complicated
world, can we return to the simplicity, the

serenity, and the guileless integrity of Jesus? There is one way which millions have found effective. It is to take a leisurely hour every day of our lives, walking with Jesus across the pages of the four gospels, and pausing to mark every word or sentence that applies to us where we are. Thus we are like a violinist who attunes his violin; Jesus keeps us in tune with the Infinite, for Jesus is the most perfectly Godlike person who ever lived. In Him we see God, and discover that God is Love. We become love by immersing ourselves in the ocean of the love of Jesus. Then the question of getting into the kingdom is settled, for we *are* in the Kingdom and the Kingdom is in us. Then death is not death but only a change of residence.